ANIMALS THAT LIVE AT THE ZOO

Welcome to the amazing world of the zoo! It's a place where you can see animals from all over the world and learn about their habitats and lifestyles. You can discover animals you may have never seen before and make new memories with your family and friends. Each animal has a unique story and reason for being in the zoo. So, let's start our journey and get ready to meet the incredible creatures that call the zoo their home!

Get ready to witness the roar of the king of the jungle! Lions are one of the most magnificent animals in the zoo. With their beautiful manes and sharp claws, they are the perfect example of strength and grace. But what makes these animals so fascinating is their social behavior. Lions live in prides, with a dominant male and several females and cubs. They hunt together and protect each other from danger. Lions also have a unique way of communicating with each other through vocalizations such as roars and growls.

One of the newest additions to the zoo was a family of polar bears. They had been rescued from the wild where they are struggling to survive due to the melting of their habitat caused by climate change. Polar bears are magnificent creatures with thick white fur and black noses. They loved to swim in their cool, blue pool and play with each other.

Elephants are one of the largest land animals in the world. They have big ears that help them keep cool in hot weather and long trunks that they use to grab food and drink water. The elephants in the zoo love to take long walks around their enclosure and play with their toys. They are very social animals and love to spend time with their herd.

Brown bears are big, furry animals that love to eat fish and berries. They have sharp claws and are very strong! They are also very playful and love to climb trees and swim in their pools. The brown bears in the zoo are very popular with the visitors, they love to put on a show by standing up on their hind legs and waving to the crowd.

Leopards are graceful big cats found throughout Africa and Asia. The leopards at the zoo are sleek and muscular, with distinctive spots. Their enclosure resembles their natural habitat, with plenty of climbing structures and hiding places.

Koala bears are small, furry animals that live up high in the trees. They are native to Australia and love to eat eucalyptus leaves. The koalas in the zoo are very sleepy animals, they spend most of their time napping in their cozy tree branches. Koalas are marsupials, which means they carry their young in a pouch. They have a unique digestive system that allows them to break down the toxins in eucalyptus leaves

Gorillas are big, powerful animals that are very intelligent. They have long arms and strong hands that they use to climb trees and eat fruit. Gorillas are also known for their social behavior and live in groups called troops. They communicate with each other using a variety of vocalizations and body language. The gorillas in the zoo love to play with their toys and climb on ropes, but they are also very gentle and love to cuddle with their zoo keepers.

Sea turtles are fascinating creatures that spend most of their lives in the ocean. They have hard, protective shells that help them stay safe from predators! They can hold their breath for a long time underwater. The visitors love to watch them swim gracefully in their habitat and learn about the importance of protecting these magnificent creatures and their habitats.

Cheetahs are the fastest land animals in the world. They have sleek bodies and long legs that help them run up to 70 miles per hour. The cheetahs in the zoo love to run and play, but they are also very shy and prefer to hide in their cozy dens when visitors are around.

Giraffes are the tallest animals in the world and have beautiful spotted coats. They use their long necks to reach up high to eat leaves on tall trees and also to watch for predators. The giraffes in the zoo love to take long strides around their enclosure and interact with visitors, some zoos even allow you to feed them!

Pandas are adorable black and white bears that are beloved all over the world. They are native to China, where they live in the forests and mountains. Pandas are known for their love of bamboo, which makes up most of their diet. They enjoy playing with toys and climbing up trees. The keepers at the zoo work hard to ensure that the pandas are healthy and happy, providing them with a variety of bamboo, toys, and plenty of space to roam around.

Chimpanzees are very clever animals that are known for their problem-solving skills. They have long arms and legs that help them swing from tree to tree. They love to eat fruit, nuts, insects, and even tree bark. The chimpanzees in the zoo are very playful and love to interact with their visitors.

Wolves are majestic creatures that live in packs in the wild. They are known for their beautiful coats and haunting howls. In the zoo, the wolves have a spacious enclosure that resembles their natural habitat, complete with rocky outcroppings and forested areas allowing them to roam. The pack is led by a dominant male and female who work together to care for their young and defend their territory.

Rhinoceroses are large, majestic animals that are found in Africa and Asia. They are known for their thick, armored skin and the large horn on their nose. Rhinoceroses are incredibly strong and can run very fast, but they are also very shy and prefer to stay hidden in their enclosures. The keepers at the zoo work hard to ensure that the rhinoceros are healthy and comfortable, providing them with a large, open enclosure with plenty of space to roam and a mud wallow to take a refreshing bath in.

Lemurs are fascinating creatures that are native to the island of Madagascar. They are known for their large eyes, fluffy tails, and lively personalities. The lemurs in the zoo are a unique species called ring-tailed lemurs, with distinctive black and white striped tails. They are very active and playful, climbing trees, leaping from branch to branch, and engaging in social grooming. The keepers at the zoo provide the lemurs with a variety of foods, including fruits, vegetables, and insects.

Kangaroos are unique animals that are native to Australia. The kangaroos at the zoo are a special species called the red kangaroo, the largest marsupial in the world. They had a spacious enclosure and are provided with a variety of foods, including grasses, leaves, and fruits. Visitors at the zoo love watching the kangaroos hop around their enclosure, using their powerful legs to propel themselves forward effortlessly. The kangaroos are fascinating reminders of the incredible diversity of life on our planet.

Zebras are beautiful animals from Africa known for their black and white stripes. The playful zebras at the zoo have a large enclosure with plenty of space to run and socialize. Keepers provide them with hay, grains, and vegetables for a balanced diet. Visitors enjoy watching them graze and interact with each other while learning about conservation and the threats they face in the wild. Zebras are a reminder of the need to protect our planet's diversity.

Hippopotamus are large animals from Africa with big mouths and sharp teeth. At the zoo, hippos live in a spacious enclosure that includes a pool to prevent dehydration and to keep their skin from being damaged by the sun. Zookeepers provide them with plenty of food options, including grass, hay, fruits, and vegetables. Visitors are amazed by their size, strength, and playfulness with each other. While learning about conservation efforts to protect their habitat loss in the wild, visitors should also be aware of their territorial nature outside of the zoo.

Snakes are fascinating creatures that can be found in many parts of the world. At the zoo, you can see different species of snakes, from the smallest to the largest, and learn about their unique characteristics. Some snakes are venomous, while others are not. Some snakes are good climbers, while others are great swimmers. Snakes play an important role in the ecosystem, as they help control the population of rodents and other pests. Although some people are afraid of snakes, they are truly remarkable animals that deserve our respect and protection.

Llamas are exciting animals known for their soft wool and gentle temperament. They are originally from South America and have been domesticated for thousands of years. They are frequently used as pack animals. You can see these friendly creatures up close and learn about their unique behaviors at the zoo. Llamas are herd animals that communicate with one another through soft hums and ear and tail movements. They are also excellent climbers and can easily navigate steep terrain. And don't forget about their eccentric personalities - llamas are known to be curious and playful, making them a delight to observe at the zoo.

Hyenas are fascinating creatures that are frequently misunderstood. They have a reputation for being vicious and scavenging for food, but they are actually skilled hunters capable of taking down large prey. At the zoo, visitors can observe hyenas' social behavior. These animals live in clans and communicate with one another through vocalizations and body language. Despite their intimidating reputation, hyenas are playful creatures who enjoy wrestling and chasing each other.

Sloths are slow-moving creatures that are native to the rainforests of Central and South America. They are known for their laid-back lifestyle and their love for sleep. At the zoo, visitors can see these fascinating animals up close and learn about their unique behaviors. Sloths are arboreal, which means they spend most of their time in trees. They move slowly and deliberately, using their strong arms to pull themselves along. Despite their slow pace, they are excellent climbers and can hang upside down from tree branches for hours on end.

Penguins are beloved creatures that live in the world's colder regions, such as Antarctica and the sub-Antarctic islands. Visitors can observe these charismatic birds up close at the zoo and learn about their unique behaviors. Penguins are flightless birds that have adapted to living in cold environments. They have a thick layer of insulating feathers that keep them warm and a layer of blubber that acts as an energy source. Penguins are also excellent swimmers, using their wings to "fly" through the water and catch fish, krill, and other small sea creatures.

Flamingos are beautiful and distinctive birds known for their bright pink feathers, long legs, and curved beaks. At the zoo, visitors can see these elegant birds wading through shallow water, using their unique beaks to filter out algae, small crustaceans, and other tiny organisms that they feed on. Flamingos are found in many parts of the world, including Africa, South America, the Caribbean, and southern Europe. They are social birds that live in large groups called colonies, where they use their calls, dances, and displays to communicate with each other and establish dominance.

Otters are playful, intelligent creatures that are native to various aquatic habitats across the world, including rivers, lakes, and coastal areas. At the zoo, visitors can watch these adorable animals swim, dive, and frolic in the water. Otters are known for their sleek, streamlined bodies, which help them navigate the water with ease. They have dense, water-repellent fur and webbed feet that aid in swimming. Otters are skilled hunters and primarily feed on fish, crustaceans, and mollusks. Their playful nature and social behavior make them a favorite among zoo visitors.

Peacocks are stunning birds known for their beautiful, iridescent tail feathers, which they use to perform elaborate courtship displays. At the zoo, visitors can see these magnificent birds up close and learn about their unique behaviors. Peacocks are native to South Asia and are a member of the pheasant family. The males are known for their striking plumage, which they fan out and shake in a captivating dance to attract a mate. Peacocks are omnivores and eat a variety of foods, including insects, seeds, and small mammals.

Camels are fascinating animals that are native to deserts in Asia and Africa. They have adapted to live in harsh environments and are known for their ability to go long periods without water. At the zoo, visitors can learn about these amazing creatures and their unique characteristics. Camels have humps on their backs that store fat, which can be converted into water and energy when resources are scarce. They also have long legs, large nostrils, and thick eyelashes to protect them from sand and dust. Camels are social animals and can often be seen interacting with each other and their keepers at the zoo.

Tigers are majestic, powerful cats that are native to Asia. They are known for their distinctive orange and black striped fur, which helps them blend into their surroundings. At the zoo, visitors can observe these awe-inspiring animals and learn about the importance of conservation efforts to protect them from habitat loss and poaching. Tigers are solitary hunters, relying on their stealth and strength to take down large prey. They are also excellent swimmers and climbers, making their enclosures at the zoo an exciting and dynamic environment.

Zoos are home to a variety of animals from all corners of the globe. The zookeepers present an opportunity for visitors to learn about the unique characteristics and behaviors of these amazing creatures, and also provide information about the importance of conservation and protecting our planet's biodiversity. From the smallest insects to the largest mammals, each animal at the zoo has a story to tell and a role to play in the intricate web of life on Earth. When visiting the zoo, children and adults will witness the wonder of the natural world and be inspired to care for and protect the countless species that share our planet.